Spiritual Intelligence
in Business

The eight pillars of 21st century business success

GW00419686

Spiritual Intelligence in Business
The eight pillars of 21st century business success

© Sarah Alexander

ISBN: 978-1-906316-51-8

Published in 2010 by HotHive Books
www.thehothive.com

A CIP record of this book is available from the British Library.

Printed in Great Britain by TJ International Ltd, Padstow, Cornwall.

Contents

About The Author –
How Spiritual
Intelligence Developed
my Business

My business life started shortly after I left university in 1983, with a BA (Hons) in Politics. It didn't take me very long to realise that I had no interest in following a career that this degree would give me. In fact I had little interest in politics at all.

My love and passion was for horses; riding them, training them and competing in many of the different equestrian disciplines. So I qualified as a riding instructor and realised that I had a gift for teaching as well, so I set up my own business as a "horsey person", teaching and training people and their horses, whilst I continued to ride and compete on my own two horses.

After a few years I bought (very cheaply) a business that was failing as a small equestrian centre and set about making it a successful enterprise. During the many years I ran these stables, I turned the business into a "top end" centre where clients could have their horses looked after and trained, and have regular training from me or one of my staff.

This business was consistently profitable right from its first year, even through the challenging economic times of the early nineties when other similar businesses were failing.

Looking back, I realise this whole business was just allowed to grow and develop organically as it naturally moved into new areas and specialties in line with my ongoing training and thinking. I knew nothing about running a business when I started out, yet things just seemed to keep working out for me the more I allowed things just to happen.

This was until 1999 when I took my finger off the pulse of that business while I went off travelling round the South Pacific for six months and then started to train for and develop a career in personal development coaching.

With my energy no longer in the business, it slowly started to go downhill and this culminated in my having to sack the person who I was employing to run the business for me and go back and run the business full time myself until it was sold in 2001.

One of the benefits I gained from my time there was the training I had received from a dressage trainer who taught a whole approach called "Ride with your Mind". I started working with her in 1987 and she taught me how to use my mind to dramatically improve my own performance and that of my horses.

I learnt from her techniques for visualisation, meditation, sport psychology, Neuro Linguistic Programming (NLP) and much about body/mind awareness. I discovered that I really gelled with these techniques, gaining huge benefit from them that I was able to pass on to my clients. What I found the most fascinating was the whole process of meditation and the awareness that one gets from stilling the mind in this way.

As a result of this I studied many different meditation practices and made meditation an important part of my life. I also trained in NLP, Stress Management, Business Coaching and qualified as a meditation facilitator.

This became my main interest and it was due to this passion for all things in the personal and spiritual development line that I realised that it would be right for me to move on from the stables and set up doing this work in its own right. So after selling the business and having my daughter, Joni, in 2001, I did exactly that.

With this business though, my approach was different. I set goals, made positive affirmations, visualised, worked hard, and did all the right things in terms of taking action and trying hard to make things happen. Despite my efforts, all I ended up with was disappointment and the feeling of just making ends meet.

After a few years of this I realised there had to be another way – and that my first approach of just letting my business grow organically had led me to success. So I changed tack, letting things happen naturally and suddenly the energy of the business started to shift towards success.

I started to gain contracts with multinational organisations that gave me some wonderful, talented managers and executives to work with, and also took me to some fantastic places both in Europe and the Far East. I also worked with some famous international sports competitors and some successful small business owners.

I still have this business today and it too has grown and developed with a natural progression. I am still aware of my need to keep letting go and allowing it all to work for me.

One relationship that I benefitted greatly from was with a dressage rider called Carl Hester. While my daughter was young and I did not have the time or focus to train my own horse, CK, regularly, I needed someone to ride and compete CK for me, which Carl did.

Carl has competed successfully in three Olympic Games and has won 51 national dressage titles to date. While CK was at Carl's stables, not only did he win six international competitions for Great Britain with Carl, but also I was able to see and know at firsthand how such a performer, who seemed to win so much, went about being so successful.

The two things that struck me most about Carl was firstly his totally relaxed and open approach to life, especially his competitive performances; I witnessed him preparing for the Athens Olympics where he finished just outside the medals and his whole approach remained relaxed and yet softly focused.

Secondly, his total willingness and enormous generosity in supporting all those who came to him for help. He had a regular stream of clients, friends and acquaintances who would all want his assistance and time, which he willingly gave.

Due to his incredibly generous nature as well as his consistent success, his training business is in great and ever-growing demand to this day.

Over this 26 year period of the highs and lows of running a business, I have learnt much. I have learnt that striving hard, setting endless goals and trying to "make" things happen just *does not work*.

It takes a lot of energy and often all you end up with is disappointment. However, allowing a business to grow in alignment with the innate flow of that business does work. Indeed this can lead you to the art of effortless accomplishment.

This book is a culmination of what I have learnt from my business failures and successes. I hope that it will inspire you too into a whole new way of thinking about how to be in business and create its success.

Sarah x

Introduction

Some say that my teaching is nonsense. Others call it lofty but impractical. But to those who have looked inside themselves, this nonsense makes perfect sense.

Tao Te Ching - Lao Tzu

As we move into the 21st century, one thing is clear. We are having to undergo a radical shift in our thinking and approach in our business world. We have come through the 20th century making many scientific and technological advances in the West. Modernisation is now equated with Westernisation and over the latter part of the 20th century much of this has spread from Western Europe and the United States to the Far East. Indeed the East has benefitted hugely from all that the West had to offer.

In the 21st century, I predict this is all about to change.

In the 21st century we in the West will gradually come to benefit from what the East has to offer, not in terms of their technological advancements, but in terms of the philosophical, spiritual and religious beliefs that are deeply embedded into the consciousness and culture of the East.

We may look at the hi-tech materialism in the Far East, the lack of concern for the environment, the poverty of the rural populations and the remnants of the Communist regimes that have underpinned many of these societies politically, and question this. Yet within these Far Eastern societies, scholars have noted that there is a growing desire, especially amongst the middle classes, to return to traditional spiritual values and practices that have been passed down through the generations, many of which were wiped out in the Communist revolution 60 years ago. The influence of the ancient religious traditions of Taoism, Buddhism and indeed Confucianism still remain and have a subtly growing effect on society today. So as Asia gradually makes a shift back to these traditional values, I predict that we in the West will follow suit and come to realise that these Eastern spiritual values have much to offer us in terms of reframing our consciousness for the 21st century.

So, this is not another book on how to run a business. This is a book that gives you new ways of looking at yourself, your business, or your role within a business and how you operate within the business world, based on timeless eastern philosophies and traditions.

The Two Religious Philosophies • • • • • • •

Firstly Buddhism, a religion that is now 2,500 years old, which is based on the personal teachings of Siddhartha Gautama and his quest for enlightenment in the 6th century BCE in Northern India. Buddhism gives us a set of spiritual and ethical principles to follow that can lead us to a life of serenity and happiness. The Buddha's teachings were not teachings received from on high; they were based on his own personal experience and practice. Buddha gave us a methodology to enable us all to fully realise our potential and put an end to our stress and suffering with his Four Noble Truths and Eightfold Path. Buddha taught the "middle way" of ethical integrity, meditative stillness and constant inquiry into our states of being.

A religion and set of philosophical beliefs that have much in common with Buddhism is Taoism, which originated in China about 2000 years ago. Taoism was considered one of the main religions of China until the Communist revolution and its philosophies and connections to the Chinese culture still permeate much of Asia to this day.

Lao Tzu, the 6th-century BCE Chinese philosopher, is accredited as the founder of Taoism. Lao Tzu spent his life in quiet contemplation as keeper of the Imperial Library, and was known for his deep wisdom. He is the writer of Taoism's key book, the *Tao Te Ching (The Way and its Power)*. For Taoists, this book is a guide to living a spiritual life in alignment with the Tao, known as "the way" or "the path".

The Tao is seen as the ultimate creative principle of the universe to which all things are connected. The Tao, regardless of our religious persuasion, guides us like a gentle current to act naturally in accord with reality. When we go with this current our innate senses take over and we find that we take the right actions at the right time with effortless skill.

Lao Tzu also gave us the concept of leadership in alignment with the Tao: "The best of all leaders is the one who helps people so that, eventually, they don't need him ... The best leader doesn't say much, but what he says carries weight. When he is finished with his work, the people say, 'It happened naturally'."

The Essence of Spiritual Intelligence • • • • •

The problem with the world is that humanity is not in its right mind.

Mahatma Gandhi

In the Western business world there seems to be a prejudice against the concept of spirituality in business. For many people the two do not mix. We have been brought up and educated to believe in facts, figures and the need for proof in all that we choose to believe. We have been trained to seek out the logical, the rational and the realistic: to believe only what the physical senses reveal to us as real in the material world.

In business we always consider the pros and cons of any business idea before we act, and we have a work ethic that maintains that the only way to succeed is to work hard.

Emphasis is put purely on "bottom line" figures and profitability, ideally short term profitability. The TV programmes *Dragons' Den* and *The Apprentice* allow us to see very successful entrepreneurs and how they operate, and we think that to be successful too, we must be and think like them. Facts and figures are the only proof we need.

Another key message we learn about success is that we must "make life happen", "take the bull by the horns", and "take massive action". We think we must fight to make things happen and try very hard at what we do because only when we have achieved our goals, will we be happy. We feel inherently that we must dominate, control, demand, direct and manipulate because this is so much a part of our culture.

Yet this whole approach makes us pushy, tense and often hard, and focuses us purely on a mentality of "get, get, get". This "getting" mentality is supported by the belief, which the media encourages us to subscribe to, that we will only be happy by getting and acquiring things. In short, it encourages us to be in a constant state of wanting.

By contrast, with Spiritual Intelligence we embody the qualities of flowing water: flowing easily and naturally on the route that we are "meant" to take, sometimes with a gentle flow and sometimes with gusto and determination; when necessary, we embrace stillness; we move through or around the rocks and boulders that block our path; in short we have the flexibility and acceptance to flow with what is.

Just like water we can get sidetracked and go off course, but if we are willing, we can return to the path set out for us which, when seen from above, has a clear destination. This destination, the sea or ocean of ultimate reality, is indeed the source of all life. From this we realise that a key aspect of Spiritual Intelligence in business is our willingness let go of our logical thinking and instead allow the flow of the water to guide us. In fact the main message is *to relax and let go*.

In Taoist thinking we flow with the Tao, the natural way that is for us to follow as we journey through life. The Tao acknowledges that things are always changing and developing and so this path through life guides us, always with perfect timing, to what we are here to do.

Its strong guiding force works through your inner thoughts and feelings, guiding you towards business ideas that are not only synergistic with your skills, talents and abilities but also those you are instinctively good and effective at.

As a result you feel a sense of ease and naturalness from your work life and are able to move through challenges with a sense that there is some higher order at play.

The *Tao Te Ching* talks of the principle of Wu Wei, or "non-doing". This "non-doing" or "non-intervention" does not mean that you literally do nothing, nor does it stop you being proactive or getting things done. It ensures though, that you act from a sense of what actions will fit best with the Tao.

Also that you do only what is required by the context of events, thus leading to greater harmony and balance in your life. This principle requires both a radical surrender and an allowing that lets things take their natural course, and this in itself requires both time and space. It is the feminine principle that embodies patience, harmony, receptivity and flow.

As Lao Tzu said in the *Tao Te Ching*, "Nature does not hurry and yet everything is accomplished."

The more we are able to give up control and become passive, the softer, more malleable, more flexible and freer flowing we become. We fear, though, that by becoming more passive we will lose out, that others will get there before us, and they will achieve more than us, earn more than us and be more successful.

To let go in this way can be extremely frightening for the Western mind. We need to develop our mental musculature to learn how not to force things to be as we want them to be, how to let go of our expectations and attachments to how we want things to turn out and how to flow with allowing things to be how they are meant to be naturally.

This "trying" and "efforting" to make things happen can often draw situations to us that are not really meant for us. The saying, "What is meant for you won't go by you", is so true. Absolutely every thing and every person that is meant to be in our lives are on their way to us, yet we try to force the Universe through the power of our minds and actions.

All we have to do is be patient and wait for the right situations to arrive. This often requires the courage and patience to do nothing.

Furthermore Taoists believe that human intervention can frequently make situations worse, so when there is a problem they do not immediately step in to try to resolve it. The *Tao Te Ching* teaches us that force merely begets more force and the harder we try to do things, the more resistance we create for ourselves.

The idea of not forcing things, encourages us to flow with the current so that our actions are natural, unforced and spontaneous. By contrast, so much of our Western stress comes from trying to interfere with, or force, the natural way of things.

We always feel we must do something in a difficult situation to stay in control. We feel if we don't act things will get worse. In fact the opposite is true. The more we are able to follow the course of non-action, and let go of the problem or issue and sense, placing it into the hands of the Tao or our sense of a Higher Power, which may be Buddha, Jesus, Allah, the Universe or indeed God, the more we can let go.

If surrendering to a Higher Power feels wrong to you, then surrender instead to the 90 per cent of your brain cells that you are not currently using!

This principle of allowing the situation to be taken care of for us and flowing with it, is perhaps the hardest to grasp. We somehow believe that the power of the Universe, which turns embryos into babies and moves the planets around the solar system, cannot sort situations and problems out for us. All we have to do is completely let go of issues, knowing that we alone can do nothing but, with the power of the Tao to assist us, we can allow ourselves to be guided to create incredible results.

If necessary, ask your sense of a Higher Power for the strength and courage to know that you are already the detached person who can handle life in alignment with the Tao, because you are. From there, know that you will only act if and when it is necessary and that economy of action is the most valuable asset you can receive when you have the trust and surrender necessary to follow the Tao.

The benefit to our sense of personal power that comes from flowing with the "is-ness" of situations is immense. We so fear being passive and letting go because we think we would become totally powerless. In truth, we are really afraid of the power that will be ours if we let go and follow the Tao.

So how do we achieve this surrendered approach in alignment with the Tao? In the next chapters are the eight pillars necessary to help you build the temple of Spiritual Intelligence in Business.

Pillar Number One – Being Inner Directed

> This is the way of direct spiritual knowing. Wholly internal, this mode is the direct experiencing of the truth through the opening of higher faculties ... there is no doubt or need of other investigations; this knowledge is beyond words, descriptions and rationalisations.
>
> 365 Tao by Deng Ming-Dao

The first and most important aspect of Spiritual Intelligence and that quality of surrendering to the Tao is that of being "inner directed".

Spiritual Intelligence within business is allowing every aspect of the business, and every decision you take pertaining to that business, to come from within you; your innate sense of intuition and inspiration that comes from your non-physical senses.

This means that everything, from the initial set up of your business, its development, expansion and change over time and all the decisions you take, including hiring staff, finding the right premises, and your sales and marketing approach, come from a sense of being guided from within.

It is allowing yourself to be guided moment to moment, in all that you do, so you become a "follower" of the guidance you receive from your sense of Tao.

You may think of the Tao as having your own Inner Guide that tells you when to speak up and act, and importantly and more often, when to be still and do nothing; what to do in every situation; and what the answers are to every decision that you have to take.

Working with your Inner Guide is especially important when you are first thinking of setting up a business. We are told when thinking of setting up a business to look for gaps in the market and then set up a business that will fill one of those gaps, supported by extensive market research and number crunching.

Yet many people now are moving out of the corporate world, either because they are forced to as a result of redundancy or because they are choosing to set up in business as entrepreneurs, doing something they really feel would bring them satisfaction and fulfilment because it is in line with their passions.

They are now realising that the self-reliant, entrepreneurial spirit that Easterners embody so well is actually going to bring them huge dividends in terms of a more relaxed lifestyle and greater job satisfaction.

So how do we work with this Inner Guide and get past that part of our mind that tells us only to do things that seem safe, sensible and, most important of all, realistic?

The reality is we have to *be willing*. We have to be willing to let go of what the logical mind tells us is the right thing to do in every situation and allow our intuitive nature to guide us in alignment with the Tao.

We are naturally "outer-directed", basing our thinking and actions on what we see, hear and know from the input of the outside world. We can become very influenced by the TV, other media and the opinions of others.

The world we inhabit, too, keeps our focus outside ourselves, keeping us constantly on the move from one thing to the next.

Also our outer directedness likes to focus us on what has worked in the past, and takes present day decisions based on that. It seems foreign to us to go within and seek the answers to our dilemmas, based on what feels right to us in the moment.

Case Study ● ● ● ● ● ● ● ● ● ● ● ● ●

Timothy is the CEO and partner in an international firm of chartered accountants, which offer a range of accountancy-related services. Timothy himself brings his Buddhist philosophies into his business management and work with clients. He is clearly a wise and insightful man whose quiet, gentle approach is very effective.

The organisation's purpose is "helping to create a positive world" for, as Timothy believes, this is the highest purpose we can have; where everyone is happy and able to see all things in a positive way.

This Buddhist thread runs through the organisation where the focus is on creating, developing and enjoying business.

Much of Timothy's work involves coaching at board level within other organisations, working with directors, both in person and in groups, helping them to take decisions based on their inner sense of knowing and giving them the confidence to rely upon it.

Despite the large sums of money spent in the corporate world on analytical techniques and training to produce logical answers, Timothy has witnessed that at the top levels of an organisation, more and more, decisions are taken at another level of thinking, often negating the analytical results.

Timothy's organisation also holds the philosophy that *we are all leaders*. Rather than suppressing individual thought, energy and ideas, as is so common in the corporate world, it is fostered through the use of in-house internet forums that give employees an opportunity to voice their views about the business and its development.

There is a specific forum for young people, the "net" generation, within the business to express their views and a Leaders' Forum, which has representatives from a cross-section of employees from different levels within the organisation, and allows them to voice their opinions on what the Board should be doing to lead the business and its clients.

Everyone is given an opportunity to join this forum at some point and their opinions are listened to and, where appropriate, acted upon.

This willingness to be guided from within the business supports Lao Tzu's philosophy of leaders as followers, where leadership sets the collective direction and initiative and then follows with subtle influence and indeed humility.

Taoist philosophies talk of the balance between the complementary forces of Yin and Yang. This is seen as the balance, regardless of our actual sex, between the masculine Yang part of our nature and the feminine Yin part.

The masculine Yang energy is the part of us that takes action in the outer world. In business it is the part of us that innovates and drives the business forward; it gets new products up and running; it carries out strategies and creates change; and it coaches and motivates people within the business.

By contrast our Yin nature is passive and receptive. It works from a sense of being inside the business looking outwards. Our Yin nature intuits the vision of the business and its projects and sees everything as part of the bigger picture; it observes, senses and listens to people, having empathy for how they are feeling; it looks at the business from the customers' and stakeholders' needs and senses how to best satisfy their needs; it seeks to empower employees, manage differences and utilise opportunities to create benefits for all.

What is important is the balance between our Yin and Yang energies. Both are complementary, so all Yang actions and initiatives must be based upon the intuitive and visionary guidance that the Yin part of our nature passively receives.

The Yang energy shouldn't just act, as is so common in the Western world. It should base all the actions it takes on the guidance it receives from the inner, receptive Yin energies.

This is how we balance our Yin and Yang and act in ways that are Spiritually Intelligent.

Even when we pray, or set intentions in alignment with the Tao, the guidance we desire as answers to our prayers and intentions will always come to us through our feminine Yin nature and sense of intuition.

Moreover it will come at exactly the right time, often in a step by step process, so that when you have completed the first step, you are then given further guidance which, when undertaken, will lead you to your next step until you reach where you are "meant" to be. In so doing you are working with your Yin and Yang nature in balance to create all that is for you.

The more you can develop a relationship with this Yin aspect of yourself by being willing to go within and ask what is next for you to do, the more your intuitive Yin nature will grow. Like any skill, the more you practise it, the more it will develop.

Suggestions for following your Inner Guide in alignment with the Tao:
Every morning be willing to connect within and ask:
Where would you have me go?
What would you have me do?
What would you have me say and to whom?
(Prayer taken from *A Course in Miracles*)

From here allow yourself to be guided and notice what seems to want to happen naturally.

Instead of seeking the opinions of others to guide your actions, be willing to go within and receive your own guidance on what actions to take.

Allow the flowing water to take you, rather than forcing the water.

If you are unsure what your focus should be as you move through any situation, use the Buddhist focus of "mette" – loving kindness in all that you do.

Pillar Number Two – Receiving Guidance from Within

Tao is within us; Tao surrounds us ... to be with Tao is harmony. To separate from Tao is disaster.
To act with Tao observe and follow. To know Tao, be still and look within.

365 Tao by Deng Ming-Dao

Our inner guidance and wisdom comes to us in four main ways. We are all capable of receiving guidance in all of these ways but our mind has habitual patterns in the way it processes information and so we will tend to favour receiving inner direction in perhaps one or two of these ways. Here are the four ways. See which one resonates with you:

Visual Guidance
Visual guidance is the ability to receive mental images and pictures, both within the mind's eye and in the world around.

People who easily receive guidance this way thrive on art, interior design, beautiful scenery and the "look" of things, from clothing to architecture. Visual guidance embraces the imagery that comes during dreams, meditation and times when we are just relaxing, contemplating or day dreaming.

Visual guidance may also come as things we are drawn to in the world around us, or which seem to leap out at us: a sign, a slogan, an internet site, a newspaper headline, a book, or an article read on impulse. One or more of these visual tweaks to our attention turn out to give us all the information we need. Yet the source that draws our attention to this guidance is still within us. All such visual messages (and indeed all guidance) will be accompanied by an intuitive gut feeling of rightness: "Yes, that's the answer I need."

Auditory Guidance ● ● ● ● ● ● ● ● ● ● ● ● ●
Auditory guidance comes either through the still, quiet inner voice within us, and more commonly as auditory messages from the world around us that we are specifically meant to hear. People who are aware of their auditory senses are those who seem to have finely tuned hearing. Musicians especially tend to find receiving auditory guidance easy.

Most often, we will pick up auditory messages by overhearing conversations that we are meant to hear, by receiving guidance (requested or not!) from other people, or even by hearing ourselves give "guidance" to others that is really meant for us. Turning on the television or radio often results in our hearing something that was "meant" for our ears. As noted above, these messages will be accompanied by that intuitive gut feeling of rightness.

Sentient Guidance ● ● ● ● ● ● ● ● ● ● ● ● ●

Sentient guidance is the ability to receive guidance through our body and emotions and through those aptly named gut feelings. Our feelings about something are literally our answers to our questions about it.

People who are naturally in tune with their feelings receive guidance easily this way. They can pick up easily what others feel: they can sense the mood in a room, the intrinsic energy of a place and people they feel drawn to or away from.

Excitement and passion will draw us towards people and activities that are meant for us; feelings of heaviness and constriction will warn us about those that are not. And often there is no feeling to do anything at all, and that is right also, to do nothing at this time except go within and know that the feeling of when to act will come to you.

Where a choice of action is being considered, imagine how you would feel when following one course, and how you would feel if you did not follow it. Positive bodily feelings signify the right choice in all that you do.

Cognitive Guidance ● ● ● ● ● ● ● ● ● ● ● ●

This is the ability to receive answers directly into our minds through ideas and thoughts that just come out of the blue. Often with this form of guidance we just know things, and we do not know how we know them! People to whom this form of guidance comes easily are naturally intelligent thinkers who like to analyse, think things through and consider all the options before making a decision. They will receive guidance directly into their mind as a series of steps to take one at a time.

All inner guidance will be positive, empowering and work as a win–win for all concerned. It often comes to us as the first thought we receive when we go within and ask what to do. What is so important though is not to "over-ride" this intuitive guidance with what seems logical, practical and the sensible thing to do.

We have to have the level of self esteem which allows us to turn away from the realistic, and follow what intuitively feels right to us, rather than talk ourselves out of it. This takes both practice and a willingness to trust your inner world, whilst still navigating your often fast-paced outer world. When you do take the recommended steps, it always feels good and right and you know intuitively that you are acting in alignment with the Tao, the natural way.

Case Study

Julia is an extremely positive and practical person. When I first met her she was a Human Resources Director for a global IT company. She is naturally a very hard working person and knows from experience that she can easily use her work ethic to over-ride her inner guidance.

In 1998 she was given a very strong message by her "universe" that her work–life balance had to change, in the form of a stress related illness that signed her off from work. As a result of the coaching she received following this illness, she realised how inspirational coaching could be and herself trained as a Business Coach. She was then offered a full time post in a training company as a Business Coach with extremely high sales targets to meet which forced her to work exclusively in the private sector. She knew deep down though, that this did not truly fulfil her desire to really serve and make a difference.

Julia left the training company in 2007 and returned to a public sector HR role only to find that she was without a job after eight days. Finding herself forced into unemployment, she realised this was another clear message that she must now step out on her own and coach the young people and those in the public sector that she felt she was really destined to help. Julia feels that if she hadn't become ill, forcing her into a change of career, and again also forced into unemployment, she would not be where she is today – working totally in alignment with her true desires and someone who makes following her Inner Guide very important, so that she does not have to have such clear "messages" again!

I think her story is common for so many people who just keep going on the corporate treadmill, ignoring what their inner guidance may be telling them, until their "universe" gives them a clear message that change is imperative and indeed

Suggestion for receiving inner guidance:

Start to retune your senses so that they are aware of your inner guidance. Notice what your attention is being drawn to by your senses.

Set intentions for your business and what you want to achieve that you "know" are in alignment with the Tao. Write down all the inner guidance that you receive to support those intentions.

Writing down your guidance in a journal helps to clarify your thinking when you have doubts as you start to see a pattern running through the inner guidance you receive.

Pillar Number Three – Meditation Practice

If waters are placid, the moon is mirrored perfectly. If we still ourselves we can mirror the divine perfectly.

365 Tao by Deng Ming-Dao

The cultivation of inner stillness and focus for the mind as advocated by both Buddhism and Taoism is essential to becoming Spiritually Intelligent. Allowing the mind to settle through meditation practice gives us the opportunity to turn away from the activity of the outer world and to go within to that place where we are receptive to our inner sense of inspiration, creativity and wonder. It allows us in short, to be receptive to the Tao and the natural way that it inspires.

Buddha's Eightfold Path encourages us to develop our inner life and internal awareness through Right Concentration, the development of mental focus. Right Concentration takes us into the domain of meditation where we can gain the benefits of unconditional peace, serenity and joy.

The importance of a daily morning meditation practice cannot be emphasised enough. It gives you both the chance to prepare your mind for the day and to consciously make the inner connection necessary to ensure that you are guided throughout your day. This inner connection may seem tenuous as you do your morning practice, yet the subtle effects of it will have an influence all day long. Just ten to thirty minutes spent every morning observing your inner world of thoughts and feelings, perhaps simply by focusing on and deepening your breath and quieting your mind, are all you need. You may instead choose a specific meditation practice that involves the quieting of what the Buddhists call "the monkey mind".

Whether you use a Buddhist mantra, listen to a meditation CD or sit and just observe the inner workings of your mind, it does not matter. What is important is the slowing of your brain wave frequencies and that sense of withdrawing from the outer world and connecting within.

When you meditate, you will notice your mind going off onto many different topics. This distraction of the mind may well persist and all you have to do is keep on witnessing the distraction without judgement, because this in itself can be strangely peaceful, then bring it back to your chosen focus. Notice also any body sensations you feel and again, don't react to them. This ability to observe without reacting will help you to move beyond the sensations, and also to not react so quickly and out of habit in your everyday life.

Another complementary and perhaps more demanding technique that you can use, is to allow yourself to fully enter into the thoughts and feelings that you are experiencing during your meditation practice.

The ability to take your focus, with a soft, present awareness, and observe whatever you are experiencing, including your negative states and feelings, allows you to pass through them and release them naturally. The key is to act as a witness to your mind processes and the emotional and physical feelings that accompany them. By allowing them to be, you find that they move to a point of being released and you are then acting in harmony with yourself.

The value of allowing your innermost thoughts and feelings to arise and be observed without judgement means that instead of being in a state of struggle with your body and emotions, you enter into a place of acknowledgement of yourself. This in turn pays huge dividends in raising your self esteem and levels of self acceptance.

To do any type of meditation all you need is a quiet place to sit upright, where you will be undisturbed by others. Ideally this should not be your bedroom, which your mind will naturally associate with sleep. As you become more practised, you will be able to extend the ability to do this in other places too, such as sitting on the train, sitting in a traffic jam, centring yourself at the beginning of a meeting and whilst walking and exercising.

Another stage of the Eightfold Path is Right Mindfulness which takes the notion of meditation a step further. It emphasises the importance of being fully present with what we say and do at all times and also being constantly aware of the effect that our words and actions have. This naturally leads us to being aware that all our words and actions are to be purely of benefit to others. This indeed places an important onus on us, not only to meditate on a regular daily basis, but also to bring that precise awareness into all that we do.

The immediacy of this awareness shows us that Enlightenment is not some far off goal that is in the future for only the chosen few. It is something that we can all attain through our willingness to cultivate a state of mindfulness and acceptance at all times.

Buddha's teaching focuses on the temporary nature or impermanence of all things and this includes our states of mind. If we can allow the moment-to-moment arising and passing of all aspects of our mind processes, both good and bad, just by witnessing them with openness and without associating into their content, then we too can experience the liberation of our minds that free us from suffering that Buddha described.

Suggestion for developing your meditation practice:
On my website www.sarah-alexander.co.uk there are both Taoist and Buddhist meditations as MP3 links that you can use free of charge.

Pillar Number Four – Work with the Laws of Causation

The mind focused can become the most powerful force we know ...
with concentration, all the various aspects of the mind can be drawn together into one superconscious mode.

365 Tao by Deng Ming-Dao

Buddha's second Noble Truth offers us the laws of causation. It is for this that perhaps the Buddha was most celebrated throughout Asia because it gave people a feeling of control over their lives and a better understanding of how and why things happened.

Today we call these laws of causation either the laws of cause and effect, the laws of karma, or quite simply "what you give out is what you get back". It sounds simple doesn't it? But in truth, given the immense power of our minds, it is an awesome responsibility. "Right View", part of the Buddha's Eightfold Path, is the recognition that everything we do counts.

Think of it is this way: the level of cause is every thought we think, every word we speak and every action we take and most importantly, the intention behind those thoughts, words and actions. The level of effect is everything we see reflected back to us in the world around us. Quite literally everything and every person in your "universe" right now is an effect of the thoughts that you have had in the past. The good news is that when you change those thoughts and the intention behind them, you have the capacity to quite literally change the world around you.

One of the few things in life that we do have total control over is the thoughts we think and the words and actions that result from those thoughts. Every time your thoughts are aligned with your "Buddha nature", the very highest and best that is within you, you are literally drawing to you all good things.

I always think of it as two sides of a room with a dividing line down the middle.

On one side of the room, say the "right" side, there are your "Buddha nature" thoughts.

Thoughts such as kindness, love, happiness, joy, generosity, forgiveness, honesty, integrity, abundance, gratitude, optimism, hope, authenticity, trust, confidence and courage.

On the left side of the room are the thoughts of your lower nature or ego self.

Thoughts of anger, frustration, impatience, hatred, envy, greed, sadness, depression, fear, anxiety, doubt, pessimism, guilt and shame.

If we stay on the right side of the room we are positively affecting the laws of causation and making ourselves magnetic to all that is good. If, however, we allow our mind to move over to the left side of the room and really associate with those thoughts, rather than just witnessing them, then we are quite literally repelling our good.

Two qualities on the "right" side of the room are worth a particular mention. Firstly gratitude, for it is said that there is a definite link between states of gratitude and the happiness we experience.

We can very easily pass through the momentum of our daily lives in a sort of unconscious haze such that we have little recall of what we have only just done and indeed what happened the day before.

The value of gratitude is that it brings our awareness back into the present moment and interrupts this unconscious haze. It helps us to recognise and acknowledge the many benefits we gain, both from people and situations, as we go about our day. It also has the benefit of imprinting our minds in a way that draws to us more situations that we can be grateful for.

Secondly the act of forgiveness, which both Taoism and Buddhism place a high importance on. Forgiveness is not only hugely beneficial in our relationships with other people, perhaps even more importantly it is also hugely beneficial for us. There is nothing that will heal our minds in such a powerful way than the ability to forgive and let go.

A Course in Miracles lists the following benefits of forgiveness: happiness, a quiet mind, certainty of purpose, and a sense of worth and beauty that transcends the world, safety, protection, gentleness and a rest, so perfect it can never be upset.

Your willingness to forgive both people, including yourself, and situations that lead to even the smallest reactions of irritation and anger within you will lead you also to the sense of unconditional peace that both these religions offer.

To return then to the laws of causation, how can we use them to help us in business? Keeping our thoughts on the "right" side of the room is certainly a major part of drawing success to us in business. However, we can take it a step further and enhance the laws of causation by knowing that whatever we wish to receive, we must be willing to first give away.

This willingness to give away the very thing we wish for seems counter intuitive and yet it is this that will make us so magnetic to exactly what we desire in business.

It is so important to remember that everything that we do, both positive and negative, is recorded and imprinted into our unconscious mind. In time, these former imprints or recordings rise up to the conscious mind and draw to us the very things that we have imprinted in our minds in the past, again both good and bad.

For Buddhists this is the real meaning of the word karma. Indeed it behoves us to be very careful about our thoughts, words, actions and intentions.

Case study

Former Buddhist monk Geshe (Master) Michael Roach was the first American to pass the 20-year course in a Tibetan monastery. He was also a founder member of the Andin International Diamond Company in New York. This business started with a $50,000 loan and over the 17 years that Roach was working in the management team, it became a global company with sales in excess of $100 million.

Today its sales are at $200 million per annum and the company has recently been bought by Warren Buffett, one of the wealthiest men in the US.

Throughout his time there Roach consistently applied Buddhist philosophies to the running of his division. In his book, *The Diamond Cutter*, which I recommend reading, he talks extensively about his use of mental imprinting to create the business success that he had at Andin.

In the book he quotes from the poem "String of Precious Jewels" by Indian master Nagarjuna, which summarises for us the states of mind that are essential for imprinting our minds for success. Here are extracts from the poem:

I'll tell you briefly the fine qualities
Of those on the path to compassion:
Giving, and ethics, patience, and effort,
Concentration, wisdom, compassion and such.

Giving is giving away what you have,
And ethics is doing good to others.
Patience is giving up feelings of anger,
And effort is joy that increases all good.

Concentration's one-pointed, free of bad thoughts,
And wisdom decides what truth really is.
Compassion's a kind of high intelligence
Mixed deep with a love for all living things.

Roach also suggests strengthening the imprinting: "The Tibetan wise men say that this should be the last part of your silent time in the morning: picturing yourself as the most successful, and wise, and compassionate person you can imagine." This will place a very strong imprint in your mind that you will inevitably become.

So what do you desire?

A steady flow of sales – be willing to be generous in every area of your business, with your time, energy and money. Even when the going is tough, keeping a generous outlook will make you magnetic to your future sales.

Good business relationships – be willing to offer help and support to others in business, including your competitors. Be pleased for their successes and be scrupulous in your dealings not only with them, but with every aspect of your business. Maintain absolute honesty, even over the smallest details, and an unwillingness to exaggerate in your business relationships – and all your relationships. This literally imprints your mind and draws good business relationships to you.

Good health – ensure the health of those around you in every area of your work and home environment.

Success – focus on assisting others to their success in every way that you can, free of the concern that you will lose out yourself by doing this.

Keep reminding yourself that literally everything you think, say and do, along with your underlying intention, is recorded by your mind and leads to an effect that appears in the future in your life.

Suggestion for positively affecting the laws of causation:

Give, give, give and you can't go far wrong.

Pillar Number Five – Seeing the Emptiness in Every Situation

There is no such thing as an objective reality.
You color everything.
If you want the highest state of being, aim for consciousness without color.

365 Tao by Deng Ming-Dao

We have talked in the previous chapter about the importance of keeping your thoughts in alignment with your "Buddha nature", the very highest and best within you.

The "room" of your thoughts I described has an important dividing line down the middle that allows your thoughts to be either magnetic or repelling to your good. At that dividing line between the two sides of the room is one thing: your interpretation of all that appears in your life – both the events in your life and the people in your life.

This interpretation is able to move us swiftly from one side of the room to the other.

We are often at the effect of the circumstances or indeed the people in our lives. We can often feel that our emotions and feelings are totally dependent on what we are experiencing.

When things appear to be going well for us and we are achieving the things we want to achieve, we feel happy, joyful and at peace. But when issues come up that trigger our negative emotional responses, suddenly we don't feel so good; we find ourselves reacting negatively and we don't seem to be able to help it.

The same can also happen with people who trigger our negative emotional responses. It seems that our projections, our internal thoughts and feelings about a person or situation, seem to exactly determine our perception of them.

So what is the way round this? How can we move through the fluctuating circumstances of our lives with seeming equanimity and calm?

One of the key ideas in Buddhist philosophy is that of "emptiness" or "non judgement". Non judgement is the ability to be able to experience a situation, or indeed a person, without placing a judgement or projection upon it. To just experience a situation exactly as it is, with no subjective opinion about it at all.

The truth is that we can all be in a situation that may seem positive to one person, and yet when seen from another person's perspective it then appears challenging.

Our recent recession gave us many examples of this. For those who were losing their jobs, or indeed their homes, the recession seemed a huge curse on them.

Yet, to those who had a surplus of wealth, it provided a means to enlarge their personal portfolios as properties, businesses and indeed labour were available at extremely reasonable prices. It provided them with incredible opportunities to expand.

The recession can be seen in many different ways, depending on our individual perspectives. Therefore, it is purely our mind's response to any situation that denotes how that situation is for us.

Our reactions to situations, and indeed to all our problems, show up the attachments that we have to life working out a certain way and also to people behaving a certain way.

The essence of Buddha's teaching is the letting go of our attachments, or at least the grasping and clinging that we have to our attachments.

Buddha teaches that this grasping we have to our attachments is the cause of our suffering. Our expectations form part of this too, for we hold expectations about everything in our life.

The more we can be aware of our attachments and expectations and let go of our grasping to them, the easier it is for things to happen in perfect alignment with the Tao. With any problem, be willing to look within and notice: what is the attachment you are holding on to? What expectation do you really want to have fulfilled in this situation? Be willing then to let them go, for as you do, you journey further on your path to liberation.

If we can acknowledge the emptiness in situations without placing our projections or attachments upon them, we are then much freer to employ our inherent creativity about how we respond to it.

The recession again was a springboard for many people to let go of employment that they were not truly happy in and an opportunity to set up a business in their own right that was totally in alignment with their own innate talents and skills, an opportunity to act in alignment with the Tao.

In reality though, we often do respond as a result of our conditioning; we do place our perceptions on a situation, depending on whether it beneficially or adversely affects us.

In fact our reactions are immediate impulses and are a result of all of our past conditioning, as well as our previous thoughts, words and actions about such issues: past causes and imprints that are now creating their effects.

What we can do, more importantly, is notice our reactions with acceptance, know that emptiness exists, and place them in the hands of our Higher Power. The more we are able to release situations and people from our projections and expectations, the more we are able to see the inherent beauty in them, the beauty both in terms of our learning and for the Tao to unfold.

Suggestions for seeing situations with non judgement:
One of the most valuable affirmations we can make in any situation that we are tempted to perceive as difficult is "out of this, only good can come".

When a problem comes up, ask your Higher Power that your thoughts, feelings, attitudes, perceptions and all attachments about this issue, and how you want it to work out, be transformed.

Ask to see the situation differently and with emptiness.

Ask to see it from the perspective of the Buddha or the Tao.

When your negative emotions come up notice them and acknowledge them in a non judgemental way. Buddha's teaching suggests acknowledging "there is anger", "there is sadness". You may then release them to your Higher Power, asking that you come to understand them and that they be transformed. Do this in the knowledge that these feelings are not the truth of you; they are merely your past pain coming up to be released.

Pillar Number Six –
The Real You

> The butterfly lives for a day.
> It comes into the world with very
> little reason except to fly and mate.
> It does not question its destiny.
> It does not engage in any
> alchemy to extend its lifespan
> or to change its lot.
> It goes about its brief life happily.
>
> 365 Tao by Deng Ming-Dao

The goal of spiritual development in Buddhism is to achieve Enlightenment or "Buddha-hood". This state of "Buddha-hood" is defined as freedom from the obstructions to our liberation, as well as to our all-knowingness.

This means that in our state of "Buddha-hood" all limitations in the form of our attachments that we hold that restrict our ability to act naturally and spontaneously, are removed.

Our path to Enlightenment is in fact the unlearning of our fear-based habits and patterns of behaviour, so that our true nature can shine forth.

It is the letting go of our "person-hood", so that all that we are capable of emerges. This, the Buddha taught, is so that we can most effectively help other sentient beings.

Taoist philosophies in the *Tao Te Ching* also support this belief, affirming that the more we act in harmony with ourselves and our true nature, the more we will achieve in all that we do, and with less effort.

The Tao naturally and easily lets our inner character shine forth integrating our inherent nature with our destined lives.

The principle of Tzu Jan means naturalness or spontaneity, or allowing that which is naturally so, both within ourselves and within a situation, without interference or conflict.

However, in the Western world, we are bombarded daily with images of what a successful business person looks like. As a result of this we try to mould ourselves and our energy into our interpretation of that.

We tend to believe that the "real" us is not what people will want or accept. We think that if we are totally authentic that people will reject us and what we have to offer. We think we have learnt what people want and we are not it.

These thought processes can shape us in a way that is not authentically who we are. We lose that element of our naturalness and this depletes our life force energy.

In truth, we won't be everyone's type and we probably won't resonate with every person – so we mustn't try to.

Overcoming these thought processes, and realising that real success is being who you truly are and expressing what you truly think and feel is another key to Spiritual Intelligence in business.

For many of us this journey of revealing our authenticity is what our growth in business becomes, especially when we run our own business in line with our innate talents and skills.

I know that from my own experience, when I started to do mostly spiritual work in my business, I was much more reluctant to share with people exactly what I did.

I didn't want to own up to being a meditation teacher, or someone who taught about different aspects of spirituality, angels and God. It all seemed too weird.

I didn't want to admit to believing that we can easily receive guidance "from above" both for ourselves and others through our intuitive impulses. Yet my growth was about owning up to these beliefs, albeit spoken with consideration for who I was talking to!

A business that has an enlightened culture where everybody radiates their own Tao energy, and are encouraged to be who they truly are, cannot help but flourish.

Encouraging people to radiate their own innate energy to the maximum is the greatest gift you can give them. The way to find this energetic vibration, and to let others find theirs, is to just let it out and be expressed to the full.

Just as little children and animals act in ways that are totally unselfconscious and spontaneous, we should do the same.

Too often though we move through our life without really checking in with ourselves and what we think and feel in situations.

The unconscious haze that we inhabit as we go about our busy day finds us with no feelings at all as we hear of yet another awful tragedy in the news; we don't stop to consider that these things are happening to real people; we just have an empty, disassociated feeling about it.

Finding the real you and letting it out involves regaining a conscious awareness of what you really think and feel about things. It involves being willing to reconnect to yourself to find out who you really are and what is welling up inside you, and then to express it.

We are meant to shine brightly, authentically and free from the barriers to our liberation. We are here with a unique path to be who we totally are and to act within the framework of total acceptance of this.

Think of it this way – all butterflies are beautiful in their own unique way. Each butterfly just is. It doesn't try to be like another butterfly. It accepts how it is unconditionally.

This same beauty and uniqueness is in you.

Suggestions for revealing the real you:
At regular intervals throughout your day, close your eyes and take your awareness within.

Notice, how do you feel emotionally and physically? What are your thought processes? Notice these without judgement and be willing to accept your inner thoughts and feelings.

Allow yourself to follow your passions and spontaneity, even initially if it is just in your time out of work. See how you behave when you are doing these things – that is the real you.

Begin to notice your attachments to being perceived a certain way. Ask your Higher Power that those areas where you are holding on to a certain self image be released. Be willing to let it go.

Be willing to be yourself in every situation and express what you think and feel without trying to be what the other person wants or expects you to be.

Pillar Number Seven – See the Oneness

True enlightenment comes from understanding the Oneness of all reality.
Such a realisation leads to a perception that all things are truly equal.

365 Tao by Deng Ming-Dao

Our Buddha nature, that part that is truly our Enlightened Self, is within us all, and yet we often choose not to see it in others.

Yet if our goal is to be the very best we can be in any situation, we must connect with the Buddha nature in others and assist them to bring it out, rather than deny it.

This Buddha nature within others is the place where we are all One. This is the place where there is no difference between "me" and "you".

It is the place that is deep within us all where we are all connected. It is the place where we let go of our perceptions that we are the centre of our reality, which Buddha refers to as our ignorance, and see ourselves as one with the world.

To be able to see everyone in this way shows that you have attained the level of openness of heart and mind that is truly your Buddha nature.

I am sure you could argue that there are times when other people are most definitely not showing us this "Buddha nature" part of themselves.

When this is so, it is because they are coming from that place of pain within them and as such deserve our compassion rather than our condemnation. This is a time of forgiveness, so that from there we can return to our sense of unity with them.

This shift in focus from a "me" orientation to a "you" orientation is another key element of Spiritual Intelligence in business. In fact it is at the core of our entire shift towards Enlightenment.

Buddha takes it even a step further and teaches us that in truth we are all "non-self", and that all there is, is Oneness and the Truth of who we are. He teaches that the life we lead is just a dream, an illusion, that one day we will wake up from.

As we live out this dream our purpose here is to keep our thinking as close to our Buddha nature as we can, so that our minds are in the spiritual world while we live out the illusion on this material plane of existence.

Suggestion for seeing the Oneness:

• Shift from focusing on "me" thinking to "you" thinking. This focus may bring up our resistance initially yet creates huge dividends in your business.

• Have a continual focus on being of service. Keep connecting with your Inner Guide in any situation, and asking how you may best serve in any situation or any person, free from your personal expectations. Buddhist mediation teacher Sharon Salzberg tells how the Dalai Lama's first though in his day is: "May every one of my actions throughout this day be for the benefit of all living things". This is a philosophy we can all use.

• To understand people fully and what they are most wanting from us, imagine stepping into the other person's persona or stepping into the other person's shoes. With your eyes see through their eyes and with your mind sense what they are thinking. What does that person want from you? How could you best meet their needs and desires? What can you do to most help them? This process, done whenever necessary with people, is not difficult and will assist you in continually having good relationships as well as doing so much to allow others to shine in alignment with their own talents and skills.

• To perceive others from a place of true Oneness, we have to accept that whatever we do to them, we are also doing to ourselves. Indeed, however we perceive them is also how we, in fact, perceive an aspect of ourselves. This is a bitter pill to swallow, as we like to deny our shadow sides – the parts of us that have negative qualities and carry out negative actions – and project them out onto others as a way of getting rid of them.

We can, however, harness the power of Oneness to ensure that all good is done to us, all help is available to us and only love is shown to us. We do that by ensuring that this is what we do to others – always doing what we can to help, to serve and to show them love. What we do to others in Oneness is what we are also doing to ourselves.

Pillar Number Eight –
The Flow of Success

Sun in heaven.
Abundance in great measure.
Supreme success
In the midst of impermanence.

365 Tao by Deng Ming-Dao

Buddha's teaching is clearly interpreted as saying that all businesses should be successful and should make money, including those run along Spiritually Intelligent lines. The commonly held belief that spirituality in business means that we should not make money is contrary to this teaching.

The focus for any business is on a time of success, a time when sales are at their maximum, goals are achieved and when what you offer is in great demand. There is a feeling of great expansion, with the business achieving its maximum output, and you feel as if you are riding a peak of a wave.

However, The *I Ching*, the Taoist book of divination, refers to this zenith period as the balmy summer days, within which we reach the longest day. This day comes at the height of our success and it is a day that can come and go almost imperceptibly.

From this point, when the sun is shining brightest and for the greatest number of hours within your business, there is a subtle shift towards the autumn of decline. This shift invariably goes unnoticed as success is still sweet and at this time we can become at our most resistant to change.

This Taoist concept of polarities – the rise and fall of business success from zenith to its opposite, nadir – can be plotted as an S curve. This curve, when seen on its side only travels in two directions – either upwards toward success or down into decline, away from the peak of success.

The *I Ching* advises us not to waste our time in trying to preserve our success. Instead have a willingness to accept with grace the forthcoming decline which will inevitably follow periods of much success. The more we can be free of the emotional attachment we have to success, the more we can allow this rise and fall as part of the natural flow of our business lives.

When we think of famous people and their business success we tend to think that they have always been successful. If, however, you read their autobiographies you will find that they too have often had to experience nadir.

Donald Trump, perhaps the most famous entrepreneur of our time, had a period in the early 1990s when he owed a total of $975 million and was facing personal bankruptcy as he had guaranteed these loans himself. Over time though he was able to find a way to pay this off and return to his former success, being quoted in the *Guiness Book of World Records* for the biggest financial turn around in history. One thing he cites in his books as important through difficult times, is having the fortitude to continue on in the face of adversity, an absolute faith that he places in God.

So while accepting the Taoist philosophies that you cannot have the zenith without the nadir, how can we move though the autumn and approaching winter months of our business with the greatest ease?

At the height of our success, as we approach our "longest day", this is a time to be going within, contemplating what is next for the business, asking for inner guidance on the next step and spending time in meditation to allow new creative ideas to be given to us. It is a time when the dreamers within a business should be doing their dreaming, spending time envisioning and planting the seeds for the next spring of growth.

This is a time of laying foundations and giving yourself the space to let new ideas grow and come to fruition within your consciousness. From here you will know what "in the world" steps are needed for you to take to set these new ideas in motion and create a new S curve for your business. You will find that this will come to you easily and naturally at the right time and will be totally in alignment with the Tao.

As we move from one business idea to the next, it allows us room to expand and grow as people, incorporating all the elements of our current talents and adding to them new skills, and new innate abilities that it is time for us to enhance.

Failure to move with the Tao in this way will inevitably lead to decline, as that S curve reaches its conclusion, back where it started.

Case Study

Chantal is a real example of someone who follows her passions and inner wisdom. With her dynamic energy she and her business partner, Kenny, set up their own radio and TV station "Passion for the Planet" in 2002 in line with her love for the environment and alternative therapies.

Over the years the radio station has grown, not just by increasing its client base of advertisers but also through Chantal's willingness to keep being guided into new areas within her existing business. Since 2002 the radio station has gone on the internet, there is TV footage available, Chantal herself now runs courses and offers coaching in promotion and marketing.

Currently she is running her own PR company, where she promotes clients with businesses that are in alignment with her thinking; all this is done with the support structure of the radio and TV station behind her. She demonstrates the need to keep moving forward in business, moving from one S curve to another, setting up the next S curve as you are just past the peak of the former.

When you have the clarity you seek, it is very tempting to start taking control and setting intentions and time frames for what you wish to have happen in line with that new business idea.

Rather than doing this, which again takes you back to demanding and controlling how things work out, hold intentions in line with Spiritual Intelligence such as:

• This project (product/service) grows from concept to completion in alignment with the Tao.
• All those involved with the project, in any way, act in alignment with their sense of inner guidance.
• All the conversations you have and actions you take to initiate and then grow this project are in alignment with your sense of inner guidance.
• The Tao guides you to the right people who can best help you to develop this idea and to the right market who can most benefit from this product.
• This project brings many benefits and positive experiences to all who are involved in it, either as a supplier or as a consumer.

From there, be willing to release all attachments and expectations you have about this product, so it can grow organically in total alignment with the Tao. Know that you will be guided as to when it is the right time to act, to initiate, develop and grow this project.

Suggestions for going with the flow of success:

Keep going within and asking your Inner Guide what is next for you. Ask for the seed of your next business idea to be placed within your heart or mind while you are at the peak of your success. From there, allow creative ideas to well up inside you and give that sense of inspiration; take action as and when you are guided.

Be willing to spend time in silence and contemplation, preferably totally away from your usual environment, observing where you are naturally being taken. This time away also helps you achieve new insights about your business and its future, as well as what strategies will work best at this present time.

Be willing also to be in the void space where you do not know where you are going next. This seems very scary to the mind, which likes to know exactly what is going to happen next, but trust you will come out of it with the clarity that you need to move forward at exactly the right time.

Conclusion – Bringing it all Together to Form the Temple of Spiritual Intelligence in Business

... if we engage solely in the frenetic activities of our daily involvements, if we seek to impose our own scheme on the natural order, if we allow ourselves to become absorbed in self centred views, the surface of our waters become turbulent. Then we cannot be receptive to Tao.

365 Tao by Deng Ming-Dao

Geshe Michael Roach believes that the very people who are drawn into business are the people who also have the strength of character to carry out what he terms "deeper practices of spirit".

The strength that it takes to set up and run a successful business is, in reality, the same inner resolve that it takes to do the inner work necessary to run the business along Spiritually Intelligent lines.

As we develop the mental musculature necessary to become Spiritually Intelligent we realise that we are embracing more and more of our feminine Yin nature.

From this we have our awareness centred within. Softly focused in the present moment, with an openness and receptivity to our inherent inner wisdom in any situation.

This Yin energy also leads us to be loving, nurturing and supportive both to ourselves and to others. In fact, the entire spiritualisation process is a feminisation process and the result of this is that we quite literally become more and more magnetic to our highest path through life in alignment with the Tao.

This process of feminisation is also our maturation process as adults. As we move from the demanding child that wants a whole list of goodies, we become a receptive adult that graciously receives from the Tao exactly what is meant for us and comes to us without any effort or struggle. The result of this is that we become more and more Spiritually Intelligent.

Case Study

Nikki is a wonderful example of using these techniques within the corporate world.

Her first corporate position in 1982 was as a Graduate Trainee when she joined a major consumer goods company.

Over the years she has moved swiftly to roles with greater and greater responsibility and influence, becoming a Human

Resources Director with a FTSE 100 multinational company by the age of 30.

She is currently a HR Director for a multinational drinks manufacturer with a global role and worldwide influence, which still continues to grow.

Nikki is always enthusiastic, and extremely generous with her time, energy and money. Her constant focus is to "make a positive difference" in all that she does.

This underlying purpose keeps her in a place of continually giving and the result is her amazing rise to success both within her current company and also her previous ones.

This success is not something that Nikki has planned – it is something that, by allowing the Tao to operate in her life, has seemingly "just happened" one step at a time.

Her story embodies so beautifully the ideas of this constant focus on giving of herself to others, and of "just allowing" in alignment with the natural order of things.

What is important is that we are able to look back on our business lives and know that the business we generated or participated in has made some real positive effect on the lives of others. For that is the true sign of success in terms of Spiritual Intelligence in business.